A Little Something

CUTE-AS-CAN-BE PATTERNS FOR WOOL STITCHERY

ROSEANN MEEHAN KERMES

Martingale®
Create with Confidence

A Little Something:
Cute-as-Can-Be Patterns for Wool Stitchery
© 2017 by Roseann Meehan Kermes

Martingale®
19021 120th Ave. NE, Ste. 102
Bothell, WA 98011-9511 USA
ShopMartingale.com

Printed in China
22 21 20 19 18 17   8 7 6 5 4 3 2 1

Library of Congress Cataloging-in-Publication Data
is available upon request.

ISBN: 978-1-60468-850-4

MISSION STATEMENT

We empower makers who use fabric and yarn to make life more enjoyable.

CREDITS

PUBLISHER AND
CHIEF VISIONARY OFFICER
Jennifer Erbe Keltner

CONTENT DIRECTOR
Karen Costello Soltys

DESIGN MANAGER
Adrienne Smitke

MANAGING EDITOR
Tina Cook

PRODUCTION MANAGER
Regina Girard

ACQUISITIONS EDITOR
Karen M. Burns

INTERIOR DESIGNER
Angie Hoogensen

TECHNICAL EDITOR
Nancy Mahoney

PHOTOGRAPHER
Brent Kane

COPY EDITOR
Sheila Chapman Ryan

ILLUSTRATOR
Sandy Huffaker

Contents

Introduction

Most of us enjoy the little extras in life—a little something sweet at the end of a meal; a little something extra slipped into our pocket as we head away from home, whether it's a heartfelt note or a little pocket money; or maybe a little something special we receive from a friend or give as a gift to ourselves. It's that last category I had in mind when I was creating the projects for A Little Something.

I grew up in a home where my mom let us be creative, as long as we cleaned up our messes! Whether it was sewing, baking, gardening, or making mosaics with tiny pieces of construction paper, she let us do it. There were always plenty of craft supplies to play with at our house. In my adult life, I've kept up the creativity with a studio I fill with bits and pieces of what I love—vintage toys, childhood treasures, favorite antique finds, ephemera, and things that make me smile. Many of those treasures are included in the photos throughout the book. And I hope as you enjoy the pictures, you'll find those little-something-extra ideas that inspire you to rethink the way you store, display, and gather your bits and pieces.

All of the projects in this book have one thing in common—they're all made using hand-dyed wool that's been washed, so it's felted and ready to use. Because the wool is felted, the edges won't fray, so you don't need to turn under any raw edges. This makes any shape easy to work with.

Most of the projects are made using scraps. Don't be afraid to use a variety of colors. A mismatched color is often the perfect color! If you don't already own scraps, you can purchase wool in small quantities—fat eighths (13" × 16") or fat quarters (16" × 26")—so you can create a stash or add to one as you go.

The appliqués are stitched by hand using embroidery floss. I use floss because it can be divided into strands. However, use the thread you love. You'll find more information about different types of thread, as well as stitch diagrams and other wool-appliqué instructions, in "Wool-Appliqué Essentials" (page 76).

One of the things I love best about working with wool is that imperfections are expected and appreciated. If your stitches are a little wonky, it just adds to the folk-art charm. Simply browse these pages to select which project you want to make. Then, begin stitching a little something for yourself or a friend. I hope whatever you make brings a smile to the face of its recipient.

~ Roseann

The pineapple has been used as a symbol of hospitality since colonial days and is still popular today. This little pouch hangs on a door to welcome guests and can be filled with decorative greenery, flowers, or herb stems.

FINISHED DIMENSIONS
6½" × 13"
(without hanging strap)

Hospitality Hanger

Materials

- 1 fat eighth (13" × 16") of blue wool for background, backing, and hanging strap
- 4" × 5½" rectangle of gold wool for pineapple
- 4½" × 4½" square of green wool for pineapple leaves
- 2" × 7½" rectangle of red wool for scalloped border
- 3½" × 3½" square of red-plaid wool for heart
- Assorted wool scraps for letters and circles
- 2½" × 7" rectangle of fusible web for letters
- Embroidery floss in gold, red, brown, green, and blue to match wool
- Freezer paper for patterns
- Chalk marker

Cutting

The appliqué patterns are on pages 9–11. Referring to "Cutting Wool Shapes" on page 78, use freezer paper to make templates for all patterns except the letters. Trace the letters onto fusible web and use an iron to press the fusible web onto the wrong side of the selected wool.

From the blue, cut:
2 rectangles, 6½" × 14"
2 strips, ¾" × 13"

From the gold, cut:
1 pineapple

From the green, cut:
1 pineapple top
1 of each leaf

From the red, cut:
1 top scallop

From the red plaid, cut:
1 heart

From scraps, cut:
1 extra-large circle
2 large circles
3 medium circles
12 small circles
Letters to spell *welcome*

Making the Hanger

For more information on any of the stitches, see page 79. Use one strand of floss throughout, unless otherwise stated.

1 Use a dry iron to adhere the bottom-scallop freezer-paper template on one short end of each blue rectangle, as shown. Cut on the line to make a scalloped end on each rectangle. To make the hanger front, measure from the center of the middle scallop and trim one rectangle to measure 13" long. To make the hanger back, trim the other rectangle to measure 13½" long, again measuring from the center of the middle scallop.

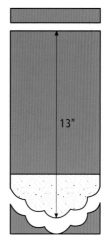
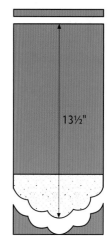

13"

13½"

Hanger front   Hanger back

2 Using gold floss and a star stitch, attach a small circle in the center of each scallop on the red top scallop. Pin the red scallop to the top edge of the hanger front, as shown **(fig. 1)**. Using one strand of red floss, whipstitch the bottom edge. Using two strands of red floss, blanket-stitch the top edge.

3 Pin the pineapple to the front piece, 2" in from each side and 2¾" up from the bottom of the center scallop. Using gold floss, whipstitch the pineapple in place.

4 Using a chalk marker, mark a line for the stitched diamond pattern as shown on the pineapple pattern (page 10). Using three 20"-long strands of brown floss, bring the needle up through the back to the front, on the outside edge of the pineapple. Following the marked line, insert the needle at the end of the line, on the outside edge of the pineapple. Knot off. Mark and stitch four lines in each direction to complete the grid.

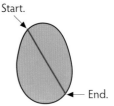

Start.

End.

5 Use gold floss to make a couching stitch over the brown floss lines, spacing the stitches about ½" apart. At each intersection, make a *plus* sign using brown floss to anchor where the lines cross **(fig. 2)**.

6 Using green floss, whipstitch the pineapple top and leaves. On the pineapple top, backstitch in the center of each leaf, ending with a small X at the tip. Using a long stitch, add two large Xs in the middle of the pineapple top **(fig. 3)**. On the bottom leaves, add three small Xs in a row near the wide end of each leaf **(fig. 4)**.

7 Position and glue baste the letters to the hanger front. Position the heart on the pineapple. Use gold floss to whipstitch the letters and the heart. Using gold floss and a star stitch, attach two small circles in the middle of the heart.

5

6

8 Layer a small, medium, and extra-large circle. Using gold floss and a star stitch, sew the circles in the center of the middle scallop on the bottom edge, sewing through all the layers. Working from the center toward the outer scallop, layer and sew small and large circles in the center of the next two scallops. In the same way, layer and sew small and medium circles in the center of the outer scallops **(fig. 5)**.

9 On the hanger back, turn the top edge under ½" to the inside and press. Using two strands of blue floss, blanket stitch the folded edge. Pin the front and back together. Using two strands of blue floss, blanket-stitch, starting below the red scallop and stitching all the way around the perimeter. Stop stitching when you reach the other side of the red scallop. Using two strands of red floss, blanket-stitch the short sides of the red scallop. The hanger top is left open.

10 Tie a knot at one end of each blue 13"-long strip and trim the other ends at an angle. (Knotting the ties will give the back more stability.) With the knot on the outside of the hanger back, pin each strip along the top edge, 2¼" in from each side. Using blue floss, stitch through all the layers and over the top of the knot **(fig. 6)**. Use the ties to hang the project from a doorknob or hook. Fill the pouch with decorative greenery, flowers, or herbs.

Embroidery Key

- - - - - - - - - Backstitch

————— Long stitch

Patterns do not include
seam allowances.

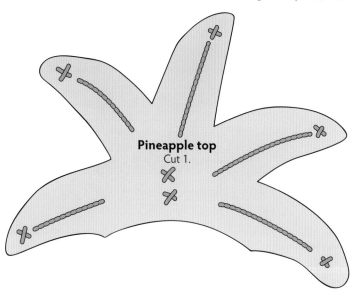

Pineapple top
Cut 1.

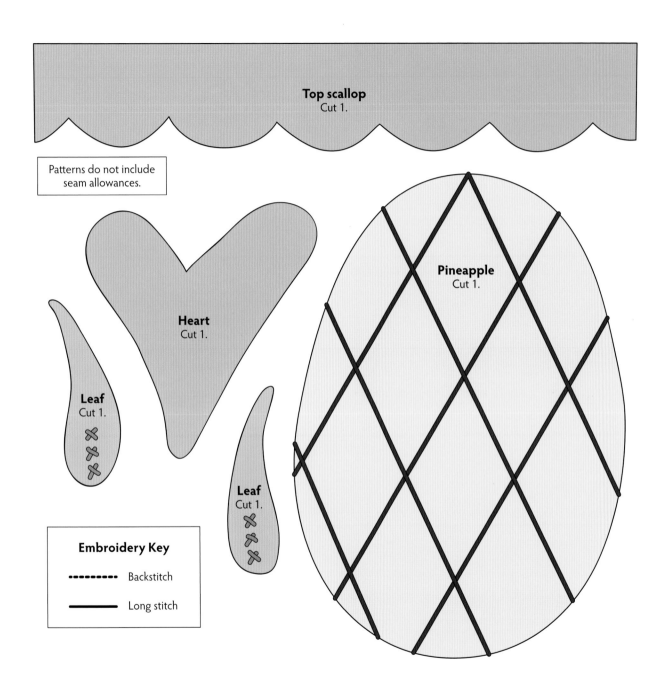

Top scallop
Cut 1.

Patterns do not include
seam allowances.

Heart
Cut 1.

Leaf
Cut 1.

Leaf
Cut 1.

Pineapple
Cut 1.

Embroidery Key

- - - - - - - - - Backstitch

———————— Long stitch

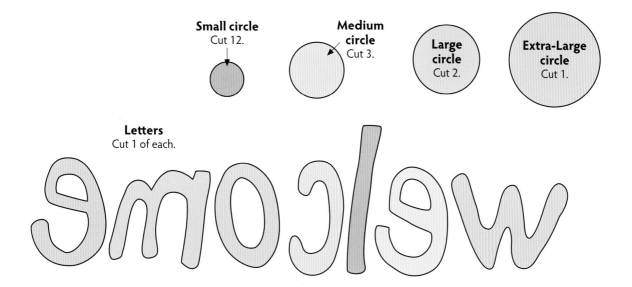

Small circle
Cut 12.

Medium circle
Cut 3.

Large circle
Cut 2.

Extra-Large circle
Cut 1.

Letters
Cut 1 of each.

Patterns do not include seam allowances. Letters are reversed for fusible appliqué.

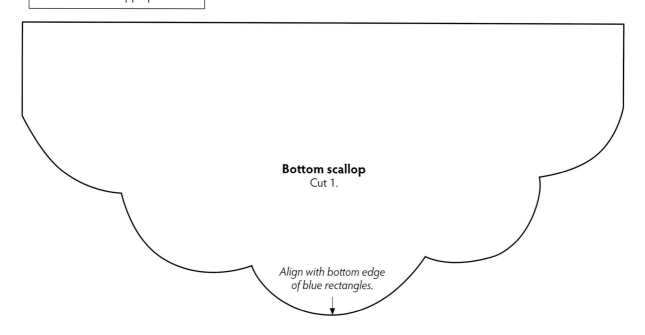

Bottom scallop
Cut 1.

Align with bottom edge of blue rectangles.

Strawberry Sewing Trio

Whip up a trio of fun that will make your time spent sewing all the more enjoyable. A cute needle keeper, pincushion, and scissors shield with fobs will make you the hit of your next retreat.

Strawberry Needle Keeper

A needle keeper is the perfect way to store your needles and pins.

FINISHED DIMENSIONS
4½" × 4¾"

STRAWBERRY
NEEDLE KEEPER
INSIDE VIEW
(FLOWER-HEAD PINS
ARE ON PAGE 20)

Materials

- 10" × 10" square of red wool for outer strawberry
- 4½" × 4½" square of pink wool for inner strawberry
- 3" × 3½" rectangle of green wool for strawberry top
- 1½" × 7" rectangle of cream wool for flowers
- 2" × 2" square of yellow wool for flower centers
- Embroidery floss in green, gold, red, and pink to match wool
- Freezer paper for patterns
- Chalk marker

Cutting

The appliqué patterns are on page 21. Referring to "Cutting Wool Shapes" on page 78, use freezer paper to make templates for all patterns.

From the red, cut:
4 strawberries

From the pink, cut:
1 inner strawberry

From the green, cut:
1 strawberry top

From the cream, cut:
5 flowers

From the yellow, cut:
5 flower centers

Making the Needle Keeper

For more information on any of the stitches, see page 79. Use one strand of floss throughout, unless otherwise stated.

1 Using green floss, whipstitch the lower edges of the green strawberry top to a red strawberry to make the front piece. Using two strands of green floss, backstitch the veins on the strawberry top as shown on the pattern.

2 On the strawberry front, use two strands of gold floss to make French knots in the lower-right area.

3 Pin a red strawberry to the back of the front piece. Using two strands of red floss, blanket-stitch around the outer edges of both pieces, starting and stopping where the green strawberry top begins. On the red strawberries, carefully trim the stem to reduce bulk, making sure to leave the green strawberry top intact.

4 Making sure the strawberry shapes are facing in the same direction as the front piece, center the pink inner strawberry on a red strawberry to make the back piece. Whipstitch the inner strawberry using pink floss. Layer the back piece on top of the front piece and use chalk to mark the outer edges of the green strawberry top.

5   Pin the remaining red strawberry to the red strawberry on the back piece. Using two strands of red floss, blanket-stitch around the edges of both pieces, starting and stopping at the chalk marks. Carefully trim away excess stem pieces on the *inner* red strawberry to reduce bulk, making sure to leave the back strawberry intact.

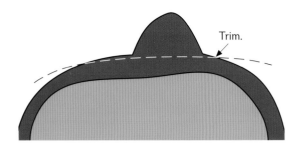

Trim.

6   Using two strands of gold floss and a star stitch, sew a yellow flower center to each flower.

7   Pin two flowers on the front near the stem. Using pink floss and a long stitch, sew from the center to the petal indentation. Make sure to insert the needle between the layers to hide the stitches. Continue around each petal. The petal edges will be loose (fig. 1).

8   In the same way, stitch one flower to the back of the needle keeper. Embroider the year next to the flower, if desired (fig. 2).

9   Pin the front and back pieces together. Use two strands of green floss and, stitching through all layers, blanket-stitch along the top edge of the leaf and stem to hold the front and back together.

10   Layer the two remaining flowers, centers facing out. Stitch the flowers together, as described in step 7, going through both layers.

11   Thread a large-eye needle with six strands of green floss. Knot one end. Slide the needle between the two flowers and take a small stitch into the back of one of them. Pull the needle through so the knotted end is hidden between the flowers. Make a stitch under a flower on the front, adjusting the length of floss so the flower unit can dangle (fig. 1). Knot off under the flower.

FINISHED DIMENSIONS
8½" long ×
2¼" wide

Strawberry Patch Pincushion

A strawberry pincushion is a timeless staple. Add one to your sewing kit!

Materials

- 6" × 7" rectangle of pink wool for pincushion body
- 3" × 6" rectangle of yellow wool for pincushion trim and flower centers
- 1" × 6" rectangle of cream wool for flowers
- 3" × 7" rectangle of red wool for strawberry
- 2" × 12" rectangle of green wool for vines, leaves, and strawberry tops
- Embroidery floss in gold, pink, green, and red to match wool
- Freezer paper for patterns
- Basting glue, such as Roxanne's Glue-Baste-It
- Cotton stuffing
- Lavender buds or crushed walnut shells

Cutting

The appliqué patterns are on page 22. Referring to "Cutting Wool Shapes" on page 78, use freezer paper to make templates for all patterns.

From the yellow, cut:
1 scallop
4 circles

From the red, cut:
1 large strawberry
3 small strawberries

From the green, cut:
1 large strawberry top
3 small strawberry tops
6 small leaves
2 vines, ⅛" × 12"

From the cream, cut:
4 flowers

Appliquéing the Pincushion

For more information on any of the stitches, see page 79. Use one strand of floss throughout, unless otherwise stated.

1. Pin the yellow scallop on the left end of the pink rectangle, overlapping the pink by ½". After overlapping the pieces, the length should be 9", as shown in the pincushion layout diagram at right. Use gold floss to whipstitch the yellow scalloped edge.

2. On the yellow piece, backstitch ⅛" from the scalloped edge using two strands of pink floss.

3. Mark a line ½" from the cut edge on both long edges. On the pink wool, center the appliqués in the middle of the pincushion.

4. Using the tip of the glue bottle, lightly draw a line for the vine. Lay one green vine on top of the glue, cutting the vine to size. Using two strands of green floss, overcast stitch the vine.

5. Using red floss, whipstitch the small red strawberries to both sides of the vine as shown in the pincushion layout diagram. Using gold floss, add three small French knots to the bottom of each strawberry.

6. Using green floss, whipstitch a small strawberry top to each strawberry. Sew the small green leaves in place using green floss and a long stitch through the center.

7. Attach three small flowers and flower centers using gold floss and a star stitch over the yellow centers. Use pink floss to make long stitches from the centers out to the petal indentations.

8. Using red floss, whipstitch the red large strawberry atop the yellow scallop. Add seven French knots in the bottom-right section of the strawberry.

9. Draw a line of glue for the vine. Lay the green vine on top of the glue, cutting the vine to size. Overcast-stitch the vine using two strands of green floss.

10. Using green floss, whipstitch the large green strawberry top to the strawberry. Then make long stitches to divide the leaf into sections.

11. Repeat step 7 to sew the remaining small flower at the end of the vine.

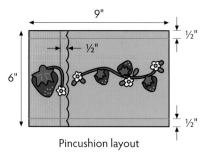

Pincushion layout

Assembling the Pincushion

1. Using the marked lines as a guide and with the right sides facing out, fold the long edges to the back, overlapping the cut edges ½". Pin in place to make a tube. The pincushion should measure 2¼" × 9".

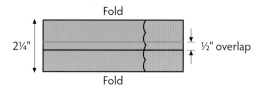

2. Using two strands of gold floss, whipstitch the back opening on the yellow scallop closed.

3. Using two strands of pink floss and beginning on the outer edge, whipstitch the pink back opening closed, stopping 2" from the yellow scallop. *Don't* cut the thread.

4. Using two strands of gold floss, blanket-stitch the short yellow end closed. In the same way, stitch the short pink end using pink floss.

5. Use the center opening to stuff each end of the pincushion with cotton stuffing. Fill the center with lavender, crushed walnut shells, or a mixture of the two. Finish stitching the opening closed.

6. Whipstitch a patch over the opening and embroider the date.

Strawberry Scissors Shield with Fobs

Keep your scissors safe! The fobs make great places to park pins and needles, too.

Materials

- 3½" × 8" rectangle of yellow wool for scissors shield and flower center
- 2¾" × 7" rectangle of red wool for strawberries
- 2½" × 13" rectangle of pink wool for ties
- 2" × 5" rectangle of green wool for strawberry tops, vine, leaves, and circle
- 1½" × 2½" rectangle of cream wool for flower
- Embroidery floss in pink, red, gold, and green to match wool
- Freezer paper for patterns
- Basting glue, such as Roxanne's Glue-Baste-It
- Cotton stuffing or batting scraps

Cutting

The patterns for the scissors shield and appliqués are on page 23. Referring to "Cutting Wool Shapes" on page 78, use freezer paper to make templates for all patterns.

From the yellow, cut:
3 scissors shields
1 large flower center
1 small flower center

From the red, cut:
2 large strawberries
1 small strawberry

From the pink, cut:
2 scallops
2 small circles
2 strips, ¼" × 13"

From the green, cut:
1 large circle
3 leaves
1 large strawberry top
1 small strawberry top
1 stem, ⅛" × 2½"

From the cream, cut:
1 large flower
1 small flower

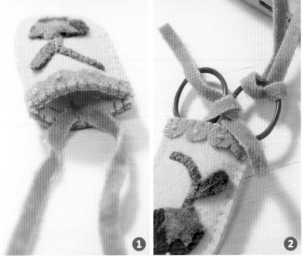

Making the Scissors Shield

For more information on any of the stitches, see page 79. Use one strand of floss throughout, unless otherwise stated. Refer to the photo on page 17 for placement.

1 Aligning the straight edges, place a pink scallop on a yellow scissors shield. Use pink floss to whipstitch the bottom edge to make the front piece. Repeat to make the back.

2 Using red floss, whipstitch the small red strawberry on the front piece. Using gold floss, add three French knots to the strawberry and a French knot in the center of each scallop.

3 On the front piece, using the tip of the glue bottle, draw a line of glue for the stem. Place the green stem on top of the glue line and trim to size. Using two strands of green floss, overcast-stitch the stem.

4 Using green floss, whipstitch the small green strawberry top to the strawberry. Attach a green leaf with one long stitch in the center.

5 Refer to the photo on page 19. On the back piece, use gold floss and a star stitch to attach both the small yellow flower center and the small cream flower, stitching through all the layers. Using pink floss, make long stitches from the center out to the petal indentation, again stitching through all layers.

6 Using green floss and a long stitch, attach a green leaf on each side of the flower.

7 Pin the third scissors shield to the back of the front piece and blanket-stitch across the top edge using two strands of pink floss. On the back piece, use two strands of pink floss to blanket-stitch across the top edge.

8 Trim one pink strip to 7" long. Fold the strip in half. Center the strip along the top edge on the inside of the back piece. Stitch in place across the center fold of the strip **(fig. 1)**.

9 Pin the front and back together. Using two strands of gold floss, blanket-stitch the edges, starting at the top and stitching all the way around the perimeter. The top edge is left open.

10 Place scissors in the shield. Tie them in place by inserting the ends of the strips through the finger holes **(fig. 2)**.

Making the Fobs

For more information on any of the stitches, see page 79. Use one strand of floss throughout, unless otherwise stated. Refer to the photo on page 17 for placement.

1 Using green floss, whipstitch the large green strawberry top onto one large red strawberry.

2 Using gold floss, make six French knots near the bottom of the strawberry **(fig. 3)**.

3 Pin the second large red strawberry to the back of the embroidered strawberry. Using two strands of red floss and starting at the edge of the green strawberry top, blanket-stitch through all layers all around the perimeter. Stop stitching when you reach the other side of the green top. Fill the strawberry with a small amount of stuffing. Using two strands of green floss, blanket-stitch around the strawberry top.

4 Center the large cream flower on top of the large green circle. Use gold floss and a star stitch to attach the large yellow flower center to the cream flower, stitching through all the layers. Using pink floss, make long stitches from the center out to the petal indentation, again stitching through all layers **(fig. 4)**.

5 Attach one end of a pink 13"-long strip to the back of the green circle. Cover the end with a small pink circle as shown in the photo at right. Whipstitch around the circle using pink floss. Attach the other end of the pink strip to the back of the strawberry, near the top. Cover the end with a pink circle and whipstitch using pink floss.

6 Loop the pink strip through one handle of the scissors with a lark's head knot.

STRAWBERRY
SCISSORS SHIELD
WITH FOBS, BACK VIEW

Flower-Head Pins

Delightful flower pins are fun to tuck into a needle keeper or to make with your friends at a retreat.

FINISHED DIMENSIONS
1⅛" in diameter (not including pin)

Materials

Yields 1 flower-head pin.

- 1½" × 1½" square of cream wool for flower
- 1½" × 1½" square of green wool for base
- Scrap of yellow wool for flower center
- Embroidery floss in gold and pink to match wool
- Freezer paper for patterns
- Flat-head pins

Cutting

The appliqué patterns are on page 22. Referring to "Cutting Wool Shapes" on page 78, use freezer paper to make templates for all patterns.

From the cream, cut:
1 flower

From the green, cut:
1 circle

From the yellow, cut:
1 flower center

Making the Flower Head

1 Using two strands of gold floss and a star stitch, attach the yellow flower center to the cream flower.

2 Center the green circle behind the flower. Using one strand of pink floss and a long stitch, sew together as follows. Insert the needle between layers to hide the knot. Bring it out along the flower center's edge. Insert it at the edge of the petal indentation. Make a small stitch on the back. Insert the needle between layers; bring it out along the flower center's edge. Stop before the last long stitch.

3 Slide the top of a flat-head pin between the circle and flower. Make the last long stitch. The stitches hold the pin head in place. Knot off; hide the knot between layers.

Patterns for Strawberry Needle Keeper

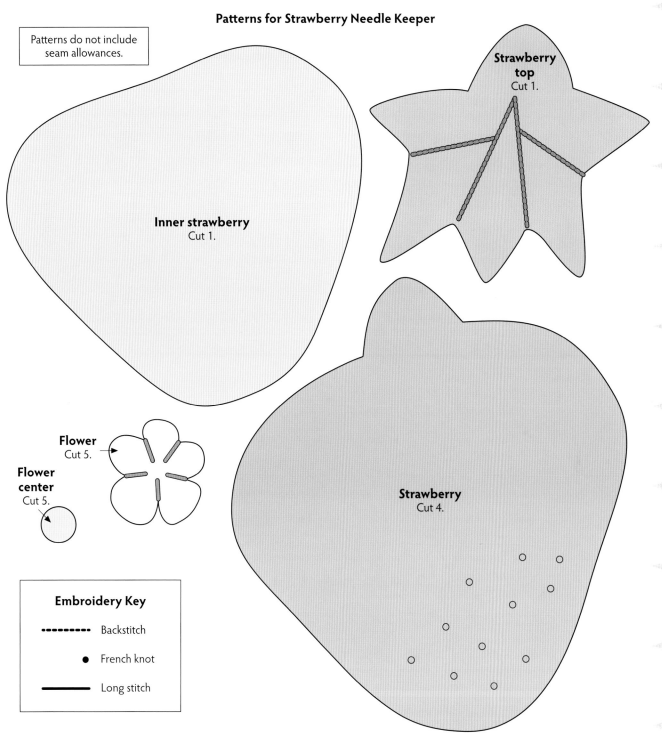

Patterns do not include seam allowances.

Strawberry top
Cut 1.

Inner strawberry
Cut 1.

Flower
Cut 5.

Flower center
Cut 5.

Strawberry
Cut 4.

Embroidery Key

- - - - - - - - -   Backstitch

●   French knot

———   Long stitch

Patterns for Strawberry Patch Pincushion

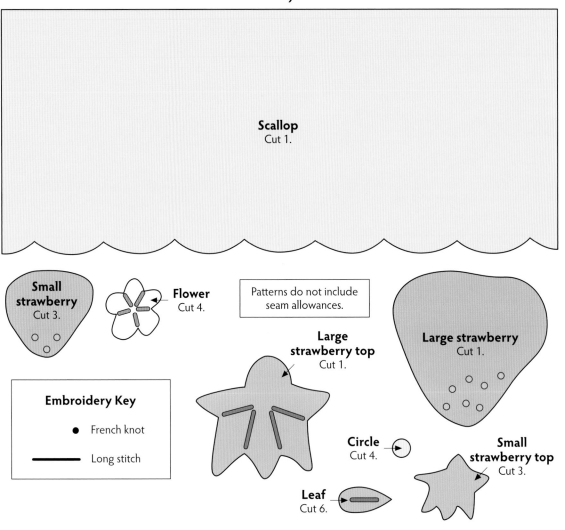

Scallop
Cut 1.

Small strawberry
Cut 3.

Flower
Cut 4.

Patterns do not include seam allowances.

Large strawberry
Cut 1.

Large strawberry top
Cut 1.

Embroidery Key

● French knot

▬ Long stitch

Circle
Cut 4.

Small strawberry top
Cut 3.

Leaf
Cut 6.

Patterns for Flower-Head Pins

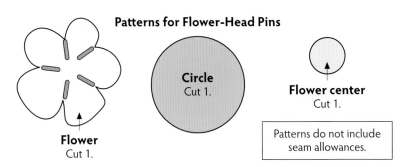

Flower
Cut 1.

Circle
Cut 1.

Flower center
Cut 1.

Patterns do not include seam allowances.

Patterns for Strawberry Scissors Shield with Fobs

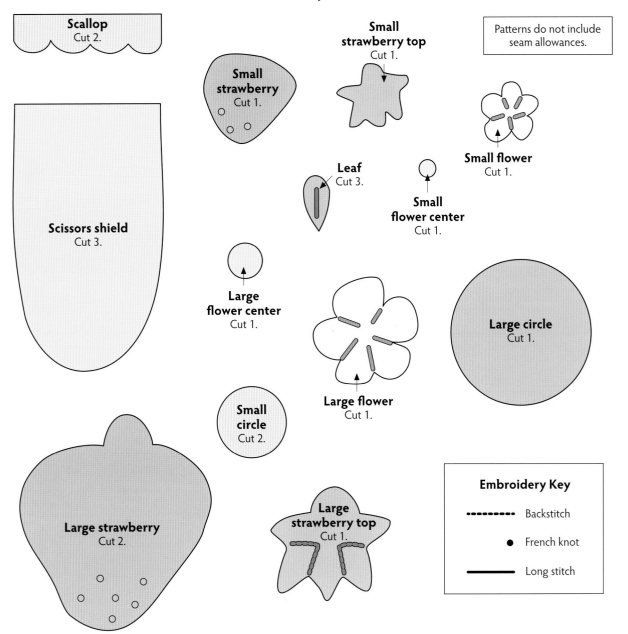

Scallop
Cut 2.

Small strawberry
Cut 1.

Small strawberry top
Cut 1.

Patterns do not include seam allowances.

Small flower
Cut 1.

Scissors shield
Cut 3.

Leaf
Cut 3.

Small flower center
Cut 1.

Large flower center
Cut 1.

Large flower
Cut 1.

Large circle
Cut 1.

Small circle
Cut 2.

Large strawberry
Cut 2.

Large strawberry top
Cut 1.

Embroidery Key

- - - - - - - - - Backstitch

● French knot

⸺ Long stitch

So fast to make, these coasters are the perfect gift for coworkers or coffee-drinking friends!

FINISHED DIMENSIONS
5" in diameter

Daisy Chain Coasters

Materials

Yields 1 coaster.

- 5" × 5" square of wool for scalloped center
- 6" × 6" square of wool for large background circle
- Assorted wool scraps for flowers, leaves, and small circles
- Embroidery floss to match or contrast with wool
- Freezer paper for patterns
- Basting glue, such as Roxanne's Glue-Baste-It

Cutting

The appliqué patterns are on pages 26 and 27. Referring to "Cutting Wool Shapes" on page 78, use freezer paper to make templates for all patterns.

From the 5" × 5" square, cut:
1 scallop

From the 6" × 6" square, cut:
1 large circle

From the scraps, cut:
3 flowers
2 leaves
6 small circles

Making the Coaster

For more information on any of the stitches, see page 79. Use one strand of floss throughout, unless otherwise stated.

1 Pin or glue baste the leaves and flowers on one side of the scallop. Using contrasting floss, star-stitch a small circle in the center of each flower.

2 Using contrasting floss, star-stitch three small circles directly opposite the flowers.

3 Using contrasting floss and a long stitch, make a V in the center of each petal.

4 Using matching floss and a long stitch, make three Xs in the center of each leaf.

5 Center the embroidered scallop on the large circle, right side facing up. Using floss that matches or contrasts with the circle, whipstitch the edges of the scallop, hiding the knots between the layers.

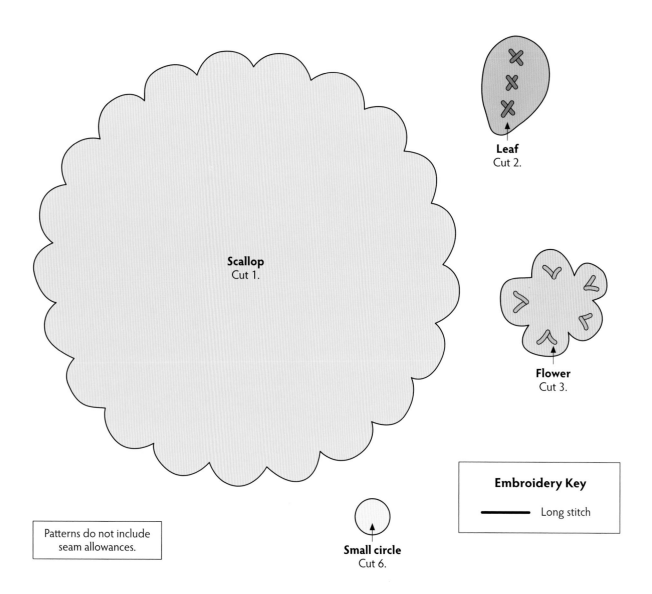

Leaf
Cut 2.

Scallop
Cut 1.

Flower
Cut 3.

Patterns do not include
seam allowances.

Small circle
Cut 6.

Embroidery Key

——— Long stitch

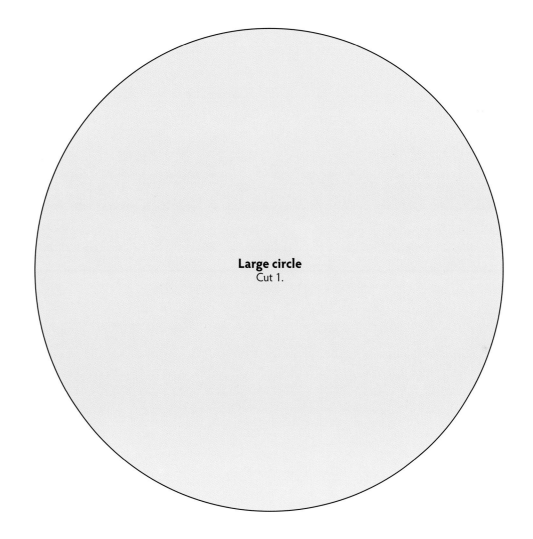

Large circle
Cut 1.

You can customize this quick candle mat with any of the appliqué motifs in this book.

FINISHED DIMENSIONS
8¼" in diameter

Bees and Buds Candle Mat

Materials

- 9" × 18" rectangle of pink wool for scallops
- 4½" × 4½" square of pink check wool for large circle
- 6" × 6" square of green wool for leaves
- Cream and black wool scraps for bee wings and bodies
- Assorted wool scraps for flower buds
- Embroidery floss in pink, green, yellow, and black to match wool
- Freezer paper for patterns
- Basting glue, such as Roxanne's Glue-Baste-It

Cutting

The appliqué patterns are on pages 30 and 31. Referring to "Cutting Wool Shapes" on page 78, use freezer paper to make templates for all patterns.

From the pink, cut:
2 scallops

From the pink check, cut:
1 large circle

From the green, cut:
12 leaves

From the cream, cut:
3 bee wings

From the black, cut:
3 bee bodies

From the scraps, cut:
8 large flower buds
8 small flower buds

Making the Candle Mat

For more information on any of the stitches, see page 79. Use one strand of floss throughout, unless otherwise stated.

1 Center and pin the pink check circle on one pink scallop. Whipstitch all around the circle.

2 Pin or glue baste the flower buds and leaves in the space between the center circle and the scalloped edge (fig. 1).

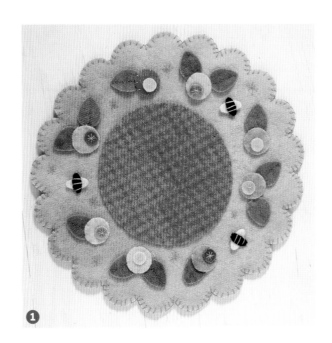

3 Use green floss to backstitch each leaf, tugging the stitches slightly to ruffle the leaf.

4 Using yellow floss, whipstitch around the large flower buds. Make a small star stitch in the center of each small flower bud.

5 Add the bees by crossing a black oval over the top of a cream oval. For the stripes, use two strands of yellow floss to make overcast stitches on the bee bodies. Stitch bee trails using two strands of yellow floss and a running stitch **(fig. 2)**.

6 Using pink floss, add random star stitches in open spaces on the pink scallop.

7 Place the remaining pink scallop on the back of the embroidered mat, matching the scallops. Pin in place. Use two strands of pink floss to blanket-stitch around the perimeter, hiding the knots between the layers.

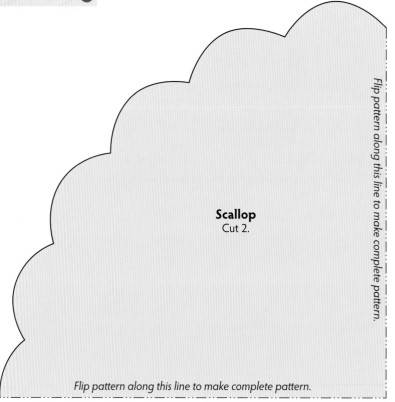

Scallop
Cut 2.

Flip pattern along this line to make complete pattern.

Flip pattern along this line to make complete pattern.

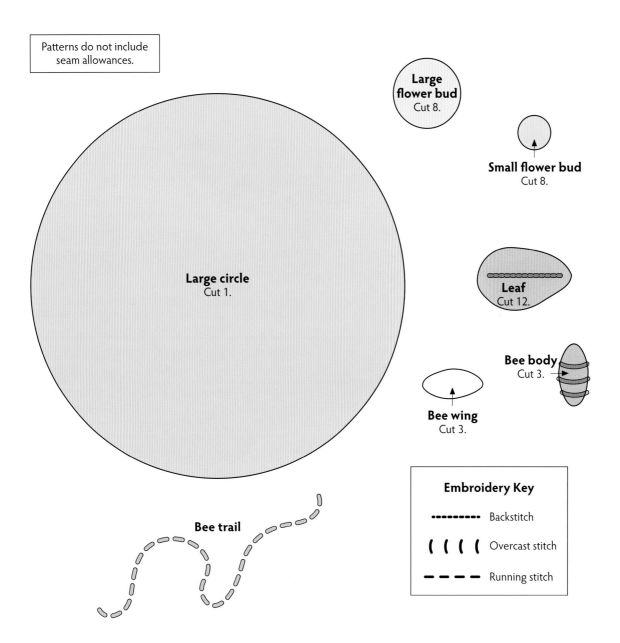

Patterns do not include seam allowances.

Large flower bud
Cut 8.

Small flower bud
Cut 8.

Large circle
Cut 1.

Leaf
Cut 12.

Bee body
Cut 3.

Bee wing
Cut 3.

Bee trail

Embroidery Key

-----------	Backstitch
((((	Overcast stitch
– – – – –	Running stitch

Embellished coffee-cup stoppers do more than keep your coffee from spilling— they look cute too!

FINISHED DIMENSIONS
1¾" in diameter

Upcycled Cup Stoppers

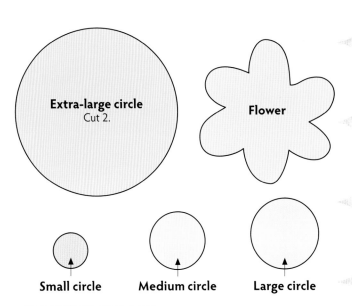

Materials

Yields 1 stopper.

- 2½" × 5" rectangle of wool for base
- Assorted wool scraps for flowers
- Embroidery floss to match or contrast with wool
- 1 plastic coffee stopper
- Freezer paper for patterns

Cutting

Referring to "Cutting Wool Shapes" (page 78), use freezer paper to make templates for all patterns below right.

From the wool rectangle, cut:
2 extra-large circles

From the scraps, cut:
Assorted flowers and circles

Making the Stopper

For more information on any of the stitches, see page 79. Use one strand of floss throughout, unless otherwise stated.

1 Referring to the photo (page 32) for ideas, layer your choice of flowers and circles on the front of one extra-large circle.

2 Again referring to the photo for guidance, stitch the flowers and circles as you choose, using star stitches, French knots, straight stitches, and Xs.

3 Place a second extra-large circle on the back of the appliquéd circle. Decide where to insert the stopper at the bottom of the circle. Using two strands of floss and hiding the knot between the layers, overcast several stitches at the bottom of the circle. Then blanket-stitch around the perimeter of the circle, stopping when you're about 1" from where you began.

4 Insert the stopper. Continue blanket-stitching until you reach the stopper. Then make several overcast stitches to secure the circles over the stopper. Knot off and hide the knot between the layers.

CREATIVE IDEA

Embroider a friend's initials on the back for a personalized gift.

Extra-large circle
Cut 2.

Flower

Small circle

Medium circle

Large circle

Patterns do not include seam allowances.

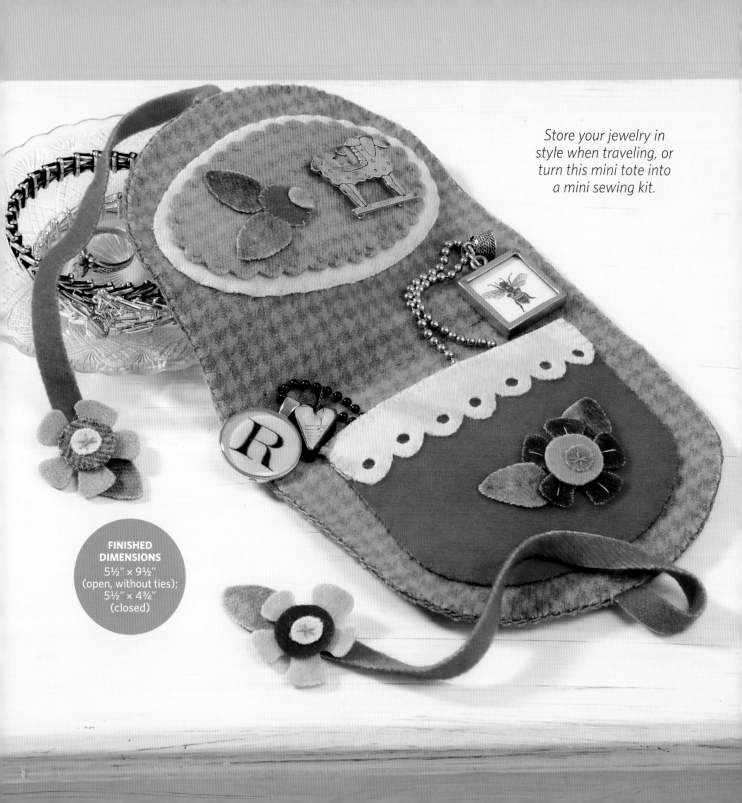

Store your jewelry in style when traveling, or turn this mini tote into a mini sewing kit.

FINISHED DIMENSIONS
5½" × 9½" (open, without ties);
5½" × 4¾" (closed)

Treasure Tote Jewelry Bag

Materials

- 8" × 13" rectangle of teal wool for outer bag and ties
- 7" × 11" rectangle of teal check wool for inner bag
- 4½" × 4½" square of red wool for pocket
- 6" × 8" rectangle of yellow wool for oval and lace trim
- 6" × 6" square of green wool for leaves
- 3" × 5" rectangle of pink wool for scalloped oval
- Assorted wool scraps for flowers and circles
- Embroidery floss in green, yellow, orange, red, pink, and teal to match wool
- Freezer paper for patterns
- ⅛" hole punch

Cutting

The appliqué patterns are on pages 38–40. Referring to "Cutting Wool Shapes" (page 78), use freezer paper to make templates for all patterns.

From the teal, cut:
2 strips, ⅜" × 13"
1 bag

From the teal check, cut:
1 bag

From the red, cut:
1 pocket

From the yellow, cut:
1 oval
2 laces

From the green, cut:
14 leaves

From the pink, cut:
1 scalloped oval

From the scraps, cut:
6 flowers
8 large circles
10 small circles

OUTSIDE VIEW

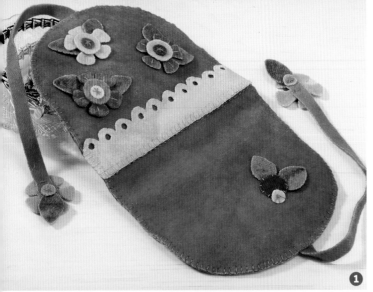

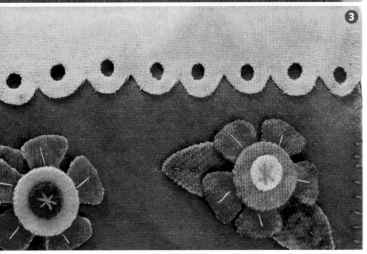

Making the Outer Bag

For more information on any of the stitches, see page 79. Use one strand of floss throughout, unless otherwise stated.

1 Fold and press the teal bag in half so it measures 4¾" × 5½". Use the creased line as a guide for placing the appliqués. Arrange three flowers on one side of the creased line; add two leaves to each flower (fig. 1).

2 Using green floss, sew a running stitch through the center of each leaf. Tug slightly to gather the leaf a bit.

3 Using yellow thread, make a long stitch in the center of each flower petal.

4 Layer a small circle on top of a large circle. Center a pair of circles on each flower. Using orange floss and stitching through all layers, make a star stitch inside the small circle. The edges of the large circles are loose.

5 On the other end of the outer bag, place a small circle on one edge of a large circle. Add two leaves and stitch them as described in step 2. Using yellow floss, whipstitch around the large circle. Using orange floss, make a French knot in the center of the small circle and three long stitches radiating from the center to the outside (fig. 2).

6 On one yellow lace, use a hole punch to make a hole in each scallop. Pin the lace to the outer bag, placing the straight edge on the creased line and making sure the scallops are even on each side. Trim the ends of the scallops even with the sides of the bag. Using one strand of yellow floss, whipstitch the bottom of the lace to the teal bag (fig. 3). Using two strands of yellow floss, blanket-stitch up one side, across the top, and down the other side.

Making the Inner Bag

For more information on any of the stitches, see page 79. Use one strand of floss throughout, unless otherwise stated. Refer to the photo on page 34 for placement.

1 On the remaining yellow lace, use a hole punch to make a hole in each scallop. Trim the top edge as indicated on the pattern. Place the lace on the red pocket, adjusting the lace so the scallops are even on each side. Trim the ends of the scallops even with the sides of the

pocket. Using one strand of yellow floss, whipstitch along the bottom of the lace. Using two strands of yellow floss, blanket-stitch across the top edge.

2 Add a flower, large circle, small circle, and two leaves to the pocket **(fig. 4)** as described in step 4 of "Making the Outer Bag" on page 36.

3 Fold and press the teal check bag in half, outer side facing in, so it measures 4¾" × 5½". Referring to the photo on page 34, on one end of the bag, pin the pocket so it's an equal distance from each side and ½" from the bottom edge. Using two strands of red floss and starting at the bottom of the lace, blanket-stitch around the perimeter of the pocket. Using two strands of yellow floss, blanket-stitch both ends of the lace. Leave the top edge open.

4 Above the pocket, on the opposite end of the bag, pin the yellow oval ½" from the top and an equal distance from each side. Using one strand of yellow floss, whipstitch around the perimeter **(fig. 5)**.

5 Add a large circle, small circle, and two leaves to the pink scalloped oval as described in step 5 of "Making the Outer Bag." Center and pin the scallop on top of the yellow oval. Using two strands of pink floss, make a French knot in the middle of each scallop.

Assembling the Bag

1 Stitch a leaf to the back of one end of each teal strip. Place a flower, large circle, and small circle on the front of each teal strip, at the same end as the leaf. Using one strand of orange floss and stitching through all layers, make a star stitch inside the small circle **(fig. 6)**. On the back of the tie, place a small circle over the stitches. Using orange floss and stitching through the top two layers only, make a star stitch inside the small circle **(fig. 7)**.

2 Center the end of a tie on each end of the inner bag. Using teal floss, anchor the ties with a few stitches.

3 Pin the inner bag to the outer bag, keeping wrong sides together and edges aligned. Using two strands of teal floss, blanket-stitch around the perimeter, hiding the knots between the layers.

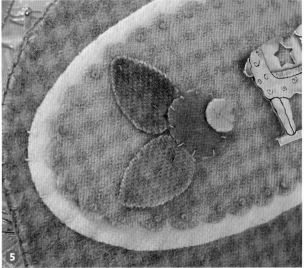

4 Fold and press the bag in half, with the inner bag on the inside. Using two strands of teal floss and stitching through all the layers, backstitch on the fold along the straight edge of the lace.

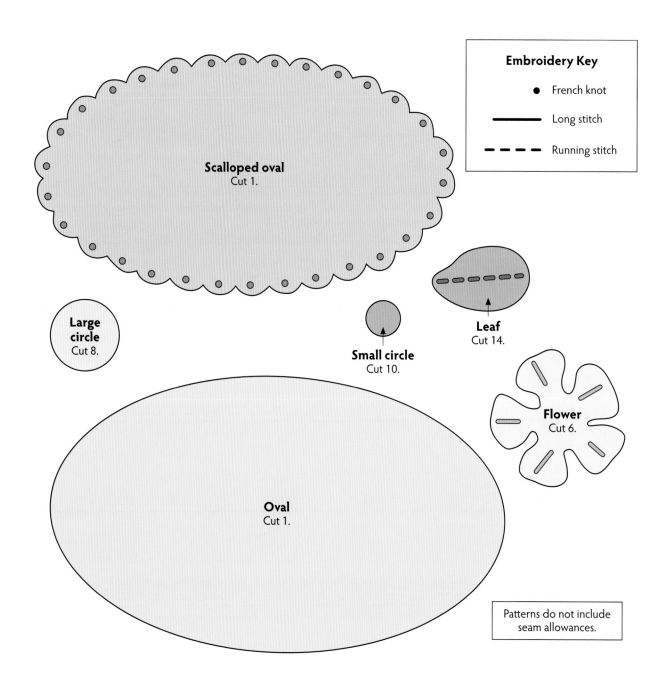

Embroidery Key

● French knot

—— Long stitch

- - - Running stitch

Scalloped oval
Cut 1.

Large circle
Cut 8.

Small circle
Cut 10.

Leaf
Cut 14.

Flower
Cut 6.

Oval
Cut 1.

Patterns do not include seam allowances.

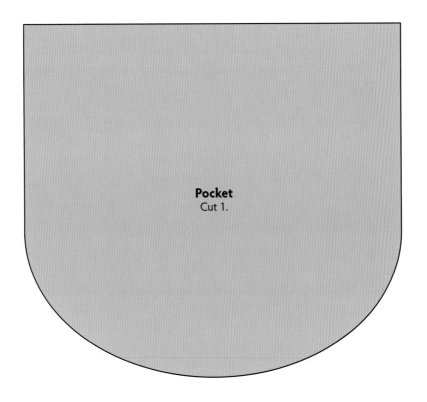

Pocket
Cut 1.

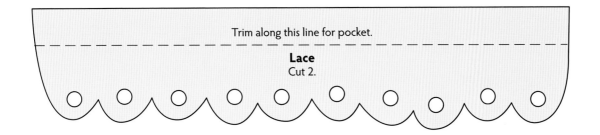

Trim along this line for pocket.

Lace
Cut 2.

Flip pattern along this line to make complete pattern.

Bag
Cut 2.

Cabin Pincushions

Like eating chips, it's hard to stop making these little pincushions once you start!

FINISHED DIMENSIONS
3½" × 3½"

Materials

Yields 1 pincushion.

- 4" × 8" rectangle of wool for pincushion front and back
- 1½" × 1½" square of wool for flower
- Assorted scraps for logs and flower center
- Embroidery floss to match or contrast with wool
- Freezer paper for patterns
- Basting glue, such as Roxanne's Glue-Baste-It (optional)
- Cotton stuffing

Cutting

The appliqué patterns are on page 43. Referring to "Cutting Wool Shapes" (page 78), use freezer paper to make templates for all patterns.

From the 4" × 8" rectangle, cut:
2 pincushion bases

From the 1½" × 1½" square, cut:
1 flower

From the scraps, cut:
1 flower center
1 log, ½" × 1½"
2 different logs, ½" × 2"
1 log, ½" × 2½"

Making the Pincushion

For more information on any of the stitches, see page 79. Use one strand of floss throughout, unless otherwise stated. Refer to the photo on page 41 for placement.

1   Arrange the logs on one pincushion base, placing them equal distance from the outer edges. Pin or glue baste in place.

2   Using matching or contrasting floss, whipstitch all around each log. Backstitch along the center of each log **(fig. 1)**.

3   Place the flower and flower center in the center of the logs. Using two strands of floss, make a star stitch over the flower center. Use one strand of floss and a long stitch to make Vs in the center of the petals to complete the pincushion front **(fig. 2)**.

4   Pin a pincushion base to the *wrong* side of the pincushion front, aligning the scalloped edges. Using two strands of floss and hiding the knot between the layers, sew a running stitch through both layers. Stitch all the way around, leaving a 2" opening for stuffing. Stuff the pincushion. Then stitch the opening closed, hiding the knot between the layers.

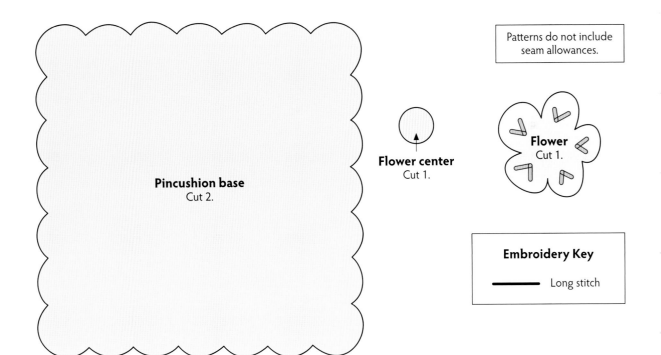

Patterns do not include
seam allowances.

Pincushion base
Cut 2.

Flower center
Cut 1.

Flower
Cut 1.

Embroidery Key

———— Long stitch

These blooms will never fade! Give a sweet wool bouquet to someone who holds a special place in your heart.

FINISHED DIMENSIONS
8½" × 11½"

Folk-Art Flowers Pillow

Materials

- 1 fat quarter (16" × 26") of teal check wool for pillow front and back
- 7" × 9½" rectangle of yellow wool for scalloped background
- 6" × 7" rectangle of green wool for stems and leaves
- 3" × 4" rectangle of teal wool for bow center and ribbon
- 2½" × 2½" square of cream wool for tag
- 5 rectangles, 2" × 2½" each, of assorted wools for tulips
- 5 rectangles, 1" × 3" each, of assorted wools for circles
- 5 rectangles, 1" × 2" each, of assorted wools for flower centers
- Embroidery floss in green, yellow, teal, and pink to match wool
- Freezer paper for patterns
- Basting glue, such as Roxanne's Glue-Baste-It
- Cotton stuffing

Cutting

The appliqué patterns are on pages 48 and 49. Referring to "Cutting Wool Shapes" (page 78), use freezer paper to make templates for all patterns.

From the teal check, cut:
2 rectangles, 8½" × 11½"

From the yellow, cut:
1 scallop

From the green, cut:
3 leaves
4 strips, ¼" × 7"

From the teal, cut:
1 left ribbon
1 right ribbon
1 bow center

From the cream, cut:
2 tags

From *each* 2" × 2½" rectangle, cut:
1 tulip (5 total)

From *each* 1" × 3" rectangle, cut:
3 circles (15 total)

From *each* 1" × 2" rectangle, cut:
1 flower center (5 total)

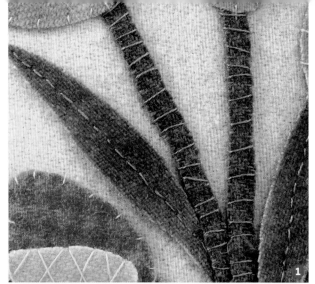

Making the Pillow Front

For more information on any of the stitches, see page 79. Use one strand of floss throughout, unless otherwise stated. Refer to the photo on page 44 for placement.

1 For the stems, use the tip of the glue bottle to lightly draw a line on the yellow scallop. Lay a green ¼" × 7" strip on top of the glue line, trimming the stem to length. Repeat to add three more stems. Pin the leaves in place, tucking them under the stems as desired. Don't stitch the leaves yet. Using two strands of green floss, overcast-stitch across the stems, moving the leaves out of the way as needed **(fig. 1)**.

2 Using yellow floss and stitching across the shape, stitch a flower center in the center of each tulip using a long stitch to make three or four large Xs. Place a tulip at the end of each stem. Whipstitch the tulips using yellow floss. You'll have one tulip left over for the pillow back. Using yellow floss and a star stitch, add three circles above each tulip **(fig. 2)**.

3 Reposition the leaves as needed. Using green floss, backstitch along the center of each leaf.

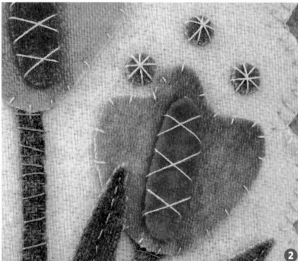

TRANSFERRING THE LETTERS

Because you can't see through wool, you can't place the pattern and wool on a light source (such as a light box or window) and trace the letters onto the wool. So, here's how I transferred the letters.

Trace the letters onto tracing paper. On the back (or unmarked) side of the paper, retrace the letters using chalk or a pencil. Lay the tracing, right side up, on the wool. Using the handle on a pair of scissors, rub the letters to transfer them from the back of the paper onto the wool.

4 Where the stems intersect, place a ribbon on each side of the intersection. Using teal floss, backstitch along the center of each ribbon. Place the bow center over the ribbon ends and whipstitch in place.

5 Center the appliquéd scallop on one teal check rectangle. Using two strands of yellow floss, blanket-stitch the scallop to the teal rectangle to make the pillow front **(fig. 3)**.

Assembling the Pillow

1 Press a corner freezer-paper template on each corner of the pillow front and trim along the curve to round the corner. Round each corner on the remaining teal check rectangle to make the pillow back.

2 Pin the pillow front and back together. Using two strands of teal floss, blanket-stitch around the perimeter of the pillow through both layers. Do not leave an opening.

3 Make a 2" vertical slit in the center of the pillow back. Stuff the pillow through the opening. Stitch the opening closed. In the same manner as before, stitch the remaining tulip and tulip center over the closure and add three circles above the tulip **(fig. 4)**.

4 Referring to "Transferring the Letters" on page 46 and using the pattern (page 49), transfer the word *Love* onto one cream tag. Using three strands of pink floss, backstitch the letters. Place the other cream tag on the back of the embroidered tag. Use one strand of yellow floss and a running stitch to sew the tags together, stitching about ⅛" all around the edges **(fig. 5)**.

5 Cut three strands of pink floss, each about 20" long. Overcast-stitch one end of the tag to the bow, making sure you have about 10" of floss on each side of the stitch. Tie the floss into a bow. Knot the ends and trim.

CREATIVE IDEA
To make a wall hanging instead of a pillow, add a sleeve or wool-strip hangers on the back.

Patterns do not include
seam allowances.

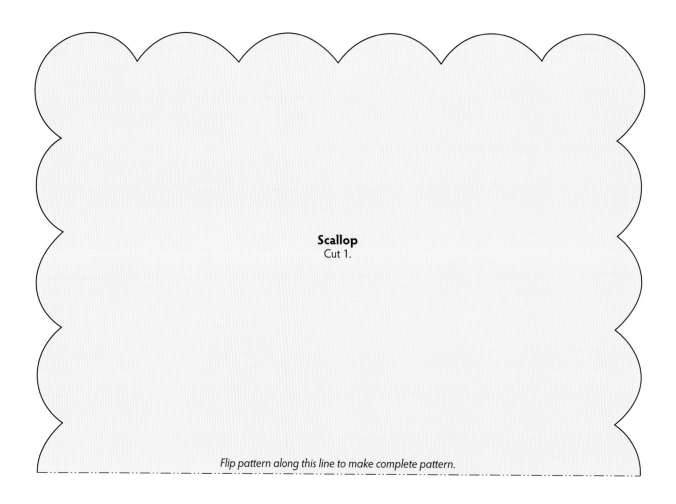

Scallop
Cut 1.

Flip pattern along this line to make complete pattern.

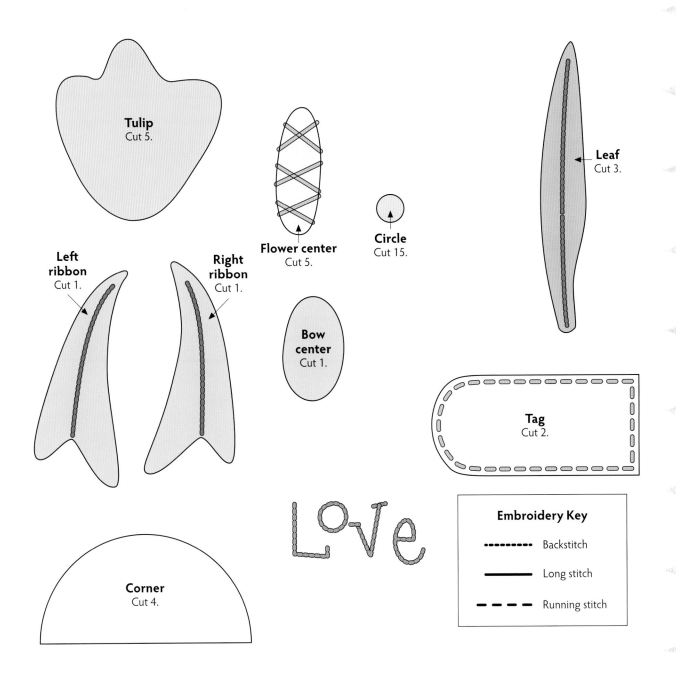

Tulip
Cut 5.

Leaf
Cut 3.

Flower center
Cut 5.

Circle
Cut 15.

Left ribbon
Cut 1.

Right ribbon
Cut 1.

Bow center
Cut 1.

Tag
Cut 2.

Corner
Cut 4.

Embroidery Key

▪▪▪▪▪▪▪▪	Backstitch
————	Long stitch
– – – –	Running stitch

Make this dazzling mini runner in just a few hours, adjusting the length to the size you need.

FINISHED DIMENSIONS
6" × 14½"

Sunny Days Runner

Materials

- 5½" × 15" rectangle of plaid wool for table runner*
- 7" × 16" rectangle of gold wool for backing*
- 2½" × 5" rectangle of gold check wool for sunflowers
- 2" × 5" rectangle of purple wool for small leaves
- 2½" × 4" rectangle of orange wool for oak leaves
- 2½" × 2½" square of turquoise wool for sunflower centers
- Assorted scraps of wool for circles
- Embroidery floss in gold to match wool
- Freezer paper for patterns

If you wish to make the runner longer or shorter than the pattern, adjust the length of the wool accordingly.

Cutting

The appliqué patterns are on page 53. Referring to "Cutting Wool Shapes" (page 78), use freezer paper to make templates for all patterns.

From the gold check, cut:
2 sunflowers

From the purple, cut:
4 small leaves

From the orange, cut:
2 oak leaves

From the turquoise, cut:
2 sunflower centers

From the scraps, cut:
12 circles

Making the Runner

For more information on any of the stitches, see page 79. Use one strand of gold floss throughout. Refer to the photo on page 50 for placement.

1 Press the scallop freezer-paper template on one short end of the plaid rectangle as shown. Cut on the line to make a scalloped end. Repeat to cut a scallop on the other end of the rectangle to make the runner front.

CREATIVE IDEA

Measure the area where you want to use the runner and cut the front wool to that length. The runner will be about ½" longer after you attach it to the runner backing and cut the scallops.

2 Arrange and pin one sunflower, one sunflower center, two small leaves, and one oak leaf on each end of the runner front.

3 Using a long stitch, make four Xs in the center of each small leaf. Make seven or eight Xs in the center of each oak leaf. Stitch large Xs around the edge of each sunflower center, stitching through all the layers.

4 On the sunflower, make a long stitch from the center to the outer edge of each petal **(fig. 1)**.

5 Place a circle between the sunflower and oak leaf on each end. Place a circle in the center of each scallop. Use a star stitch to attach the circles **(figs. 1 and 2)**.

6 Press the table-runner top and then center and carefully pin it to the gold rectangle.

7 Whipstitch all around the perimeter of the front, being careful to not pull the stitches too tight **(fig. 3)**. Tie off and hide the knot between the layers. Press.

8 Using scissors, carefully cut the gold backing a scant ¼" from the edges of the front. Press.

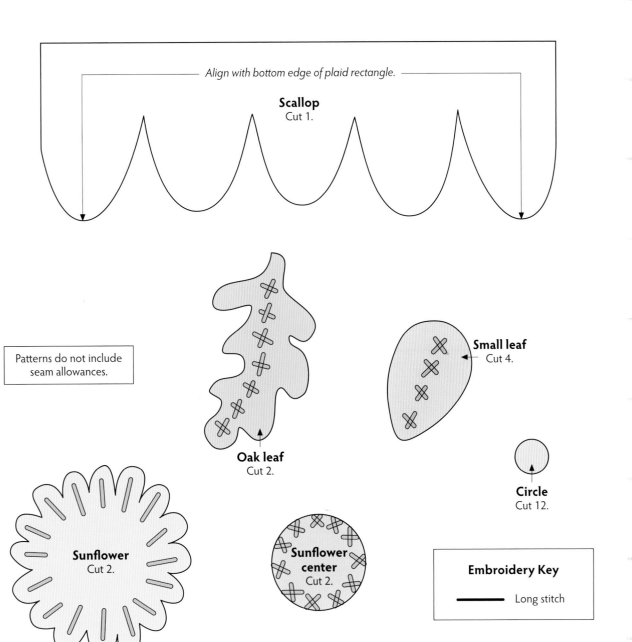

Align with bottom edge of plaid rectangle.

Scallop
Cut 1.

Patterns do not include
seam allowances.

Small leaf
Cut 4.

Oak leaf
Cut 2.

Circle
Cut 12.

Sunflower
Cut 2.

**Sunflower
center**
Cut 2.

Embroidery Key

——— Long stitch

Autumn is my favorite time of year in Minnesota. Celebrate the abundance of the season with this bright, cheerful little wall hanging.

FINISHED DIMENSIONS
7" × 10¼"

Autumn Abundance Wall Hanging

Materials

- 1 fat eighth (13" × 16") of purple wool for front, back, and hanging strips
- 8" × 10" rectangle of mustard wool for top band, basket, and circles
- 2½" × 5" rectangle of red wool for large sunflower, circle, small sunflower, and oak leaf
- 4" × 4" square of bright gold wool for small sunflower, circles, and oak leaf
- 4" × 4" square of orange wool for small sunflowers, circle, and oak leaf
- 2" × 3" rectangle of green wool for small leaves
- 2" × 2½" rectangle of black wool for crow
- 2" × 3" rectangle of teal wool for basket band and circles
- Assorted wool scraps in autumn colors for circles, acorns, and small sunflower
- Embroidery floss in gold, purple, orange, black, and brown to match wool
- Freezer paper for patterns

Cutting

The appliqué patterns are on pages 58 and 59. Referring to "Cutting Wool Shapes" (page 78), use freezer paper to make templates for all patterns.

From the purple, cut:
2 rectangles, 7" × 11"
2 strips, ¾" × 14"

From the mustard, cut:
1 basket
1 top band, 1¼" × 7"
4 large circles

From the red, cut:
1 large sunflower
1 curved oak leaf reversed
1 small sunflower
1 small circle

From the bright gold, cut:
1 large circle
1 straight oak leaf
1 small sunflower
2 small circles

From the orange, cut:
1 curved oak leaf
3 small sunflowers
1 small circle

From the green, cut:
8 small leaves

From the black, cut:
1 crow

From the teal, cut:
1 basket band
3 small circles

From the scraps, cut:
5 small circles
3 acorns and 3 acorn caps
1 small sunflower

Making the Front

For more information on any of the stitches, see page 79. Use one strand of floss throughout, unless otherwise stated. Refer to the photo on page 54 for placement.

1   Place the scallop freezer-paper template on one short end of each purple rectangle, as shown. Cut on the line to make one scalloped end on each rectangle. Measuring 10¼" from the scallop edge, trim the top edge on each rectangle. Set aside one trimmed rectangle to use for the back.

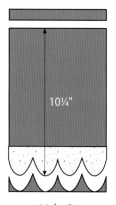

10¼"

Make 2.

2   Place three small sunflowers on the gold band, and then center a small circle on each. Place a small bright gold circle between each sunflower. Using one strand of gold floss, whipstitch the circles to the flowers. Then use a long stitch to make small Xs inside each circle, stitching through all layers. Using two strands of purple floss and a star stitch, attach the gold circles (fig. 1).

3   Pin the appliquéd band to the top of one purple rectangle from step 1. Using two strands of purple floss, blanket-stitch the bottom edge of the band to the purple rectangle.

4   Center a large mustard circle on the front of each bottom scallop. Using gold floss, whipstitch around the large circles. Place a small circle in the center of each large circle. Attach the small circles using gold floss and a star stitch (fig. 2).

5   Center the basket on the front. Using gold floss, whipstitch around the perimeter of the basket, including the inside edge of the handle to secure it. Whipstitch the teal basket band to the basket. Using gold floss, make four pairs of long stitches on the band.

6 Referring to the photo on page 54, arrange and pin the small leaves and oak leaves on and around the basket. Add the small and large sunflowers and circles, along with the crow.

7 On the large sunflower, use gold floss to whipstitch all around the gold circle. Then make long running stitches horizontally and vertically through the center for texture. Using orange floss, make long stitches from the center circle outward, placing the stitches between the sunflower petals.

8 On the small sunflowers, use gold floss to whipstitch around the small circles. Then use a long stitch to make small Xs inside each circle, stitching through all of the layers.

9 On each oak leaf, use orange or purple floss to stitch a double row of running stitches along the center of the leaf. Overcast stitch the stems. Using orange floss and a backstitch, stitch a line in the center of each small leaf.

10 Using black floss, whipstitch around the perimeter of the crow.

11 Position the acorns and caps on the front, placing a different color cap on each acorn. Using brown floss, whipstitch around the acorns and caps, attaching a cap to each acorn.

12 Using orange floss, stitch groups of three French knots randomly around the basket to represent bittersweet.

Assembling the Wall Hanging

1 Pin the back to the wrong side of the appliquéd front. Using two strands of purple floss, blanket-stitch all around the perimeter through all layers.

2 Fold both purple 14"-long strips in half to make two 7"-long strips. On the back of the wall hanging, place the strips 1½" in from each side. Use a running stitch to sew each strip in place, stitching across the fold in the strips and through the back layer of the hanging only. Use these strips to hang your masterpiece on the wall (fig. 3).

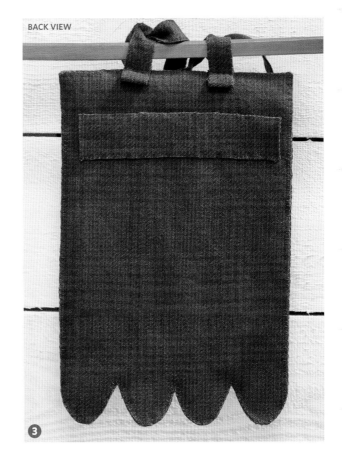

BACK VIEW

❸

CREATIVE IDEA

For a rustic look, use a stick as a hanger. Add a 1½" × 6" hanging sleeve to the back, stitching through only one layer so that no threads show on the front.

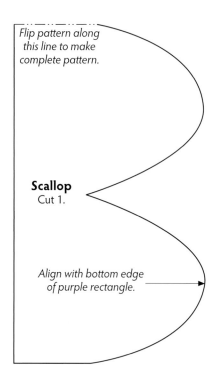

Flip pattern along this line to make complete pattern.

Scallop
Cut 1.

Align with bottom edge of purple rectangle.

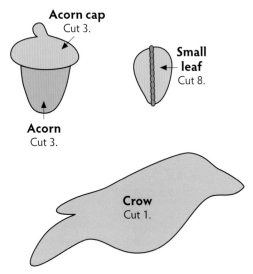

Acorn cap
Cut 3.

Small leaf
Cut 8.

Acorn
Cut 3.

Crow
Cut 1.

CREATIVE IDEA

Make use of extra wool shapes you cut out. Layer and stitch them to opposite ends of narrow wool strips; then tie them onto a basket handle or display hanger.

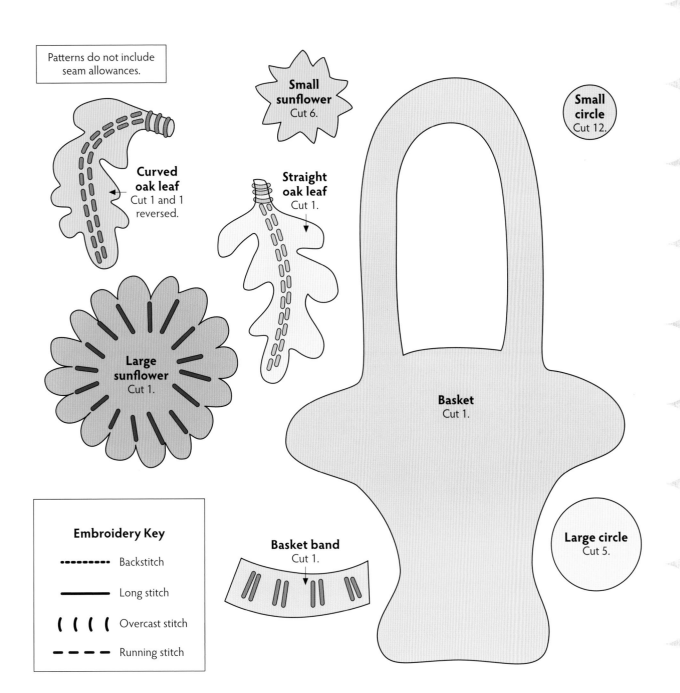

Patterns do not include seam allowances.

Curved oak leaf
Cut 1 and 1 reversed.

Small sunflower
Cut 6.

Straight oak leaf
Cut 1.

Small circle
Cut 12.

Large sunflower
Cut 1.

Basket
Cut 1.

Embroidery Key

- - - - - - - - -   Backstitch

───────   Long stitch

((((Overcast stitch

- - - - -   Running stitch

Basket band
Cut 1.

Large circle
Cut 5.

Cell Phone Satchel

*Dual duty . . . artfully carry your phone or your
school supplies in this handy little pouch!*

**FINISHED
DIMENSIONS
4" × 6"**

Materials

- 4" × 15" rectangle of teal wool for satchel body*
- 1½" × 10" rectangle of yellow wool for zigzag trim
- 2½" × 2½" square of red wool for flower
- Assorted wool scraps for flowers and leaves
- 36" length of leather cording for strap
- Embroidery floss in yellow, teal, and green to match wool
- Freezer paper for patterns

Measure the dimensions of your cell phone and adjust the size of the teal rectangle if needed.

Cutting

The appliqué patterns are on page 63. Referring to "Cutting Wool Shapes" (page 78), use freezer paper to make templates for all patterns.

From the yellow, cut:
2 trims

From the red, cut:
1 flower

From the scraps, cut:
2 large leaves
4 small leaves
3 large circles
3 medium circles
6 small circles

BACK VIEW

Making the Satchel

For more information on any of the stitches, see page 79. Use one strand of floss throughout, unless otherwise stated. Refer to the photo on page 60 for placement.

1 Fold and press the teal rectangle in half so it measures 4" × 7½". Unfold it. On each short end, fold and press 1½" to the right side to make the front and back flaps. The teal rectangle should now measure 4" × 12".

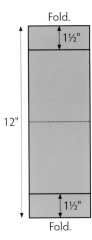

Fold.

1½"

12"

1½"

Fold.

2 Tuck a yellow trim under the front and back flaps, leaving ½" of the zigzag edge exposed. Using teal floss, whipstitch the straight edge on both flaps, stitching through all three layers.

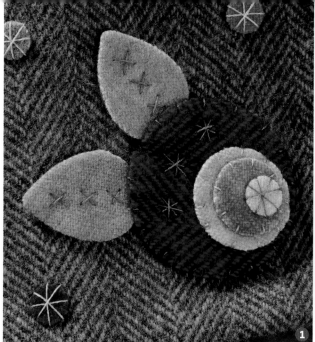

3 Layer the red flower and large leaves on the front of the bag. Layer a small, medium, and large circle and place them off center on the red flower. Using teal floss, whipstitch around the flower. Using yellow floss, whipstitch around the medium and large circles **(fig. 1)**.

4 Using teal floss and a star stitch, make three small stars on the red flower. Attach the small circle using a star stitch. Using green floss and a long stitch, make three large Xs along the center of each leaf **(fig. 1)**.

5 Arrange a small, medium, and large circle on the front flap. Add two small leaves. Using yellow floss, whipstitch around the medium and large circles. Attach the small circle using a star stitch. Using green floss and a long stitch, make three large Xs along the center of each leaf **(fig. 2)**.

6 Using yellow floss and a star stitch, attach three small circles to the satchel front.

7 Repeat step 5, stitching two small leaves and a small, medium, and large circle to the back of the satchel as shown in the photo on page 61.

8 Fold the satchel in half, wrong sides together. Using two strands of teal floss, blanket-stitch all the way around the perimeter, starting at the top edge on one side. Blanket-stitch the teal edges together, stitching underneath the yellow trim, leaving the trim loose along the sides. Stop stitching when you reach the top edge on the other side, leaving the top edge open **(fig. 3)**.

9 Make a knot in each end of the cording. Position one end of the cording on each inside corner, adjusting the length as needed. Use an overcast stitch to sew the ends in place **(fig. 4)**.

Patterns do not include seam allowances.

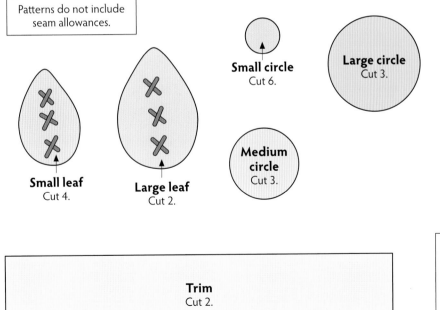

Small circle
Cut 6.

Large circle
Cut 3.

Small leaf
Cut 4.

Large leaf
Cut 2.

Medium circle
Cut 3.

Flower
Cut 1.

Trim
Cut 2.

Embroidery Key

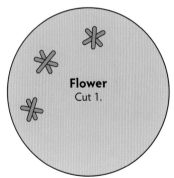

—————— Long stitch

Fill this bag
with treats or
posies and
hang to enjoy.

**FINISHED
DIMENSIONS**
7½" × 7"
(not including
ties)

Spring Bouquet Bag

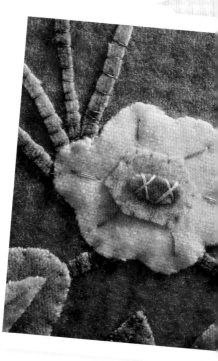

Materials
- 1 fat eighth (13" × 16") of pink check wool for bag body and ties
- 6" × 8" rectangle of green wool for stems and leaves
- 2" × 3½" rectangle of bright yellow wool for daffodil, ball flower center, and tulip center
- 2" × 3½" rectangle of pink wool for ball flower and circles
- 2½" × 2½" square of lavender wool for tulip and circles
- Assorted scraps of gold, orange, cream, and black wool for flower centers and bee
- Embroidery floss in yellow, green, orange, cream, lavender, and pink to match wool
- Freezer paper for patterns
- Basting glue, such as Roxanne's Glue-Baste-It

Cutting
The appliqué patterns are on pages 68 and 69. Referring to "Cutting Wool Shapes" (page 78), use freezer paper to make templates for all patterns. For the bag, trace the bag top and bottom onto freezer paper, joining the top and bottom patterns as indicated on the patterns to make the complete bag.

From the pink check, cut:
2 bags
2 strips, ¾" × 14"

From the green, cut:
3 large leaves
6 small leaves
6 strips, ⅛" × 8"

From the bright yellow, cut:
1 daffodil petals
1 tulip center
1 ball flower center

From the pink, cut:
1 ball flower
8 circles

From the lavender, cut:
1 tulip
3 circles

From the gold, cut:
1 daffodil cup

From the orange, cut:
1 daffodil center

From the cream, cut:
3 lily of the valley
1 oval

From the black, cut:
1 oval

Appliquéing the Bag Front
For more information on any of the stitches, see page 79. Use one strand of floss throughout, unless otherwise stated. Refer to the photo on page 64 for placement.

1 On the bag front and back, fold the top scalloped edge over about 1½" to the right side of the bag. Using two strands of yellow floss, blanket-stitch around the scallops on the front and back, stitching only through the scallops and not the bag. Set the back aside.

2 On the bag front, center a lavender circle and two small leaves on each scallop. Using green floss, make a long stitch in the center of each leaf. Using orange floss, make a French knot in the center of each circle. Then use yellow floss to make three long stitches from the center to the outside of the circle as shown in figure 4 on page 67.

1

2

BACK VIEW

3   Use the tip of the glue bottle to lightly make six glue lines for the stems. Lay a green strip on top of each glue line, cutting the strips to length. Using green floss, make overcast stitches across each stem.

4   Position the yellow daffodil petals on the bag front, covering the ends of the stems. Using yellow floss, whipstitch around the petals. Center the gold daffodil cup on the petals and whipstitch around the edge using orange floss. Center the orange daffodil center on the daffodil cup and stitch two large Xs over the top using two strands of yellow floss. Using orange floss, make one long stitch on each daffodil petal **(fig. 1)**.

5   On three stems, position a lily of the valley at the end of each stem. Using cream floss, whipstitch around each flower. Use two strands of yellow floss to make a large lazy daisy in the center of each flower. Using orange floss, make a French knot in the notch of each flower **(fig. 2)**.

6   Place the tulip at the end of a stem. Using lavender floss, whipstitch around the flower. Position the tulip center in the middle of the tulip. Using yellow floss, whipstitch around the tulip center. Using two strands of orange floss, make a long stitch and French knot on the

tulip center as shown on the pattern. Then make three long stitches from the petal edges toward the center of the tulip.

7 Position the ball flower on the bag front. Using pink floss, whipstitch around the flower. Position the flower center on the flower. Using yellow floss, whipstitch around the flower center. Using pink floss, make a French knot in the center of the flower center.

8 Arrange three pink circles at the end of one stem. Position five pink circles at the end of the remaining stem. Using yellow floss, make a star stitch over the top of each pink circle.

9 Position the large leaves between the flowers. Using green floss, whipstitch the edges of each leaf. Make a running stitch through the center of each leaf and three long stitches as shown on the pattern.

10 For the bee, place a cream oval horizontally and a black oval vertically over the top of the cream oval. Use two strands of yellow floss to make three long stitches, beginning and ending on either side of the black body. Stitch a bee trail behind the bee using two strands of cream floss and a running stitch (fig. 3).

Assembling the Bag

1 Pin the bag front to the bag back, wrong sides together. Using two strands of pink floss, blanket-stitch the layers together, starting at the top edge on one side. Stop stitching when you reach the top edge on the other side, leaving the top edge open.

2 Tie a knot at the end of each pink ¾"-wide strip. Using an overcast stitch and stitching right above the knot, sew a tie to each side of the bag (fig. 4).

3 Tie the two strips together, adjusting the length as needed. Cut the ends of the strips at an angle.

CREATIVE IDEA
Fill a small bottle half full with water and add flowers to it. Tuck a paper towel into the top of the bottle and carefully put the bottle inside the bag to display a fresh bouquet.

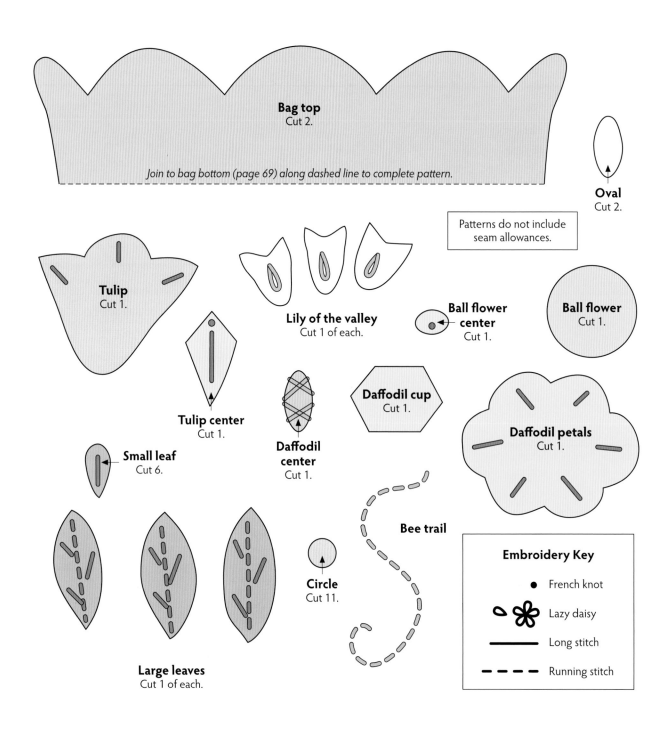

Bag top
Cut 2.

Join to bag bottom (page 69) along dashed line to complete pattern.

Oval
Cut 2.

Patterns do not include seam allowances.

Tulip
Cut 1.

Lily of the valley
Cut 1 of each.

Ball flower center
Cut 1.

Ball flower
Cut 1.

Tulip center
Cut 1.

Daffodil center
Cut 1.

Daffodil cup
Cut 1.

Daffodil petals
Cut 1.

Small leaf
Cut 6.

Bee trail

Large leaves
Cut 1 of each.

Circle
Cut 11.

Embroidery Key

- French knot
- Lazy daisy
- ⎯⎯ Long stitch
- ‐ ‐ ‐ Running stitch

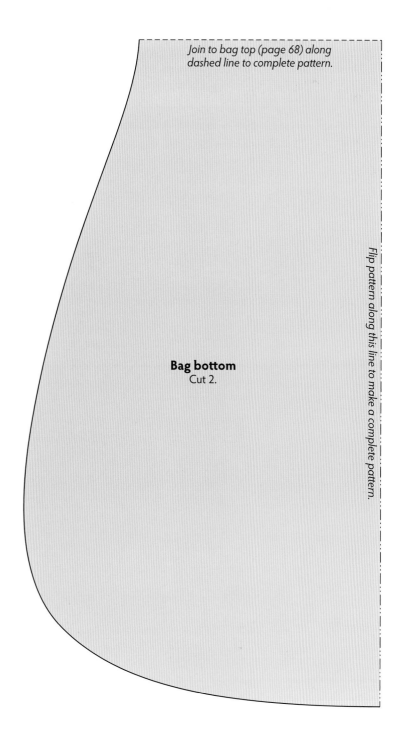

Join to bag top (page 68) along dashed line to complete pattern.

Bag bottom
Cut 2.

Flip pattern along this line to make a complete pattern.

FINISHED DIMENSIONS
9" × 11"
(without frame)

Use up your wool
scraps in this
cheerful wall art.
Add a colorful
frame to complete
the look.

Home Sweet Home Wall Art

Materials

- 1 fat eighth (13" × 16") of eggplant wool for foundation
- 8" × 9" rectangle of turquoise wool for background
- 5" × 10" rectangle of red wool for scallops, rickrack, daisy, and large leaf
- 2½" × 2½" square of yellow wool for scallop flower
- 1½" × 6" rectangle of green wool for rickrack and circle
- Assorted wool scraps for penny tongues, circles, hearts, leaves, and letters
- Embroidery floss in turquoise, red, yellow, and green to match wool
- 6" × 7" rectangle of fusible web for letters
- Freezer paper for remaining patterns
- Basting glue, such as Roxanne's Glue-Baste-It
- Frame with 7¼" × 9¼" interior opening*
- Double-sided tape

If the frame doesn't come with cardboard, you'll also need two 8½" × 10½" pieces of cardboard (or pieces slightly smaller than the size of the back opening on the frame). The appliquéd piece will be wrapped around one piece of cardboard. The other piece will be used to cover the back of the project. Or, you can wrap the appliquéd piece around foamcore and cover the back with craft paper.

Cutting

The appliqué patterns are on pages 74 and 75. Referring to "Cutting Wool Shapes" (page 78), use freezer paper to make templates for all patterns except the letters. Trace the letters onto fusible web and use an iron to press the letters onto the wrong side of the selected wool. Note that if your frame opening doesn't measure 7¼" × 9¼", you may have to adjust the size of some pieces to accommodate your opening.

From the red, cut:
1 scallop
1 rickrack
1 daisy
1 large leaf

From the yellow, cut:
1 scallop flower

From the green, cut:
1 rickrack
1 medium circle

From the scraps, cut:
3 penny tongues
3 large circles
4 medium circles
5 small circles
4 hearts
1 large leaf
3 small leaves
Letters to spell *home sweet home*

Appliquéing the Design

For more information on any of the stitches, see page 79. Use one strand of floss throughout, unless otherwise stated. Refer to the photo on page 70 for placement.

1 Fold and press the eggplant rectangle in half vertically and horizontally to establish centering lines. Center the frame over the rectangle, making sure that at least 2" extends beyond the frame opening on all sides. As you work, periodically lay the frame over the piece to make sure the layout is correct.

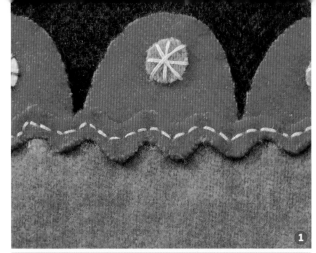

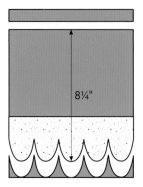

2 Place the scallop freezer-paper template on one short end of the turquoise rectangle, as shown. Cut on the line to make a scalloped end. Measuring from the edge of the scallops, trim the rectangle to measure 8¼" long.

8¼"

3 Fold the turquoise background in half vertically and place it on the eggplant foundation, aligning the center folds. Tucking the straight edge of the red scallop ¼" under the top edge of the turquoise piece, pin the red scallop onto the eggplant foundation. Using red floss, whipstitch only the scalloped edge of the red piece. Do not stitch along the straight edge. Using turquoise floss, whipstitch the bottom edge of the turquoise scallop to the eggplant rectangle.

4 Pin the red rickrack over the straight edge of the red scallop. Using two strands of yellow floss, backstitch through the center of the rickrack to attach it. Trim the rickrack even with the edges. Using two strands of yellow floss and a star stitch, add a small circle in the center of each red scallop (fig. 1).

5 Place a penny tongue along the left side of the turquoise background, ¾" below the rickrack. Add the remaining two penny tongues, spacing them about ½" apart, with the straight edges aligned with the turquoise edge. Using yellow floss, whipstitch around each tongue. Layer a medium and a large circle on the ends of each tongue. Using yellow floss, whipstitch around each circle (fig. 2).

6 Starting on the left, center a heart on the first four turquoise scallops. Using yellow floss, whipstitch around each heart.

7 To the right of the penny tongues, position and glue baste the letters to the turquoise background, evenly spacing the words. Using turquoise floss, whipstitch around each letter.

8 Cut the green rickrack into five sections for stems. Pin the stems along the right edge of the turquoise background; the ends of the stems will be tucked under the leaves and flower.

9 Using turquoise floss and a running stitch, attach the yellow scallop flower. Center the red daisy on the scallop flower. Using yellow floss and a running stitch, stitch through the center of the petals on the red daisy. Center a medium circle on the red daisy. Using two strands of turquoise floss, make a star stitch over the circle (fig. 3).

10 Pin the leaves along the right edge of the turquoise background, adjusting the position of the stems as needed. Using green floss, whipstitch the stems. Using two strands of green floss and a long stitch, make Xs down the center of each leaf. On the red leaf, make five Xs to attach the leaf to the background. Note that the pointed ends of two of the leaves will extend underneath the frame (fig. 4).

Finishing the Wall Art

1 On the left and right sides, whipstitch the turquoise background to the eggplant foundation.

2 Place a piece of cardboard (or foamcore) on the wrong side of the eggplant foundation. Fold the edges of the wool over the cardboard, making sure the fabric is taut but not distorted. Secure the fabric with double-sided tape.

3 Cover the back of the project with another piece of cardboard (or craft paper) and secure it with double-sided tape. Or, you can cover the back with another piece of wool and whipstitch around the perimeter using matching floss. Insert the project into the frame and use the clips that came with the frame to secure the project.

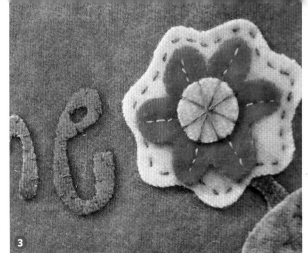

3

4

CREATIVE IDEA

Find frames at a dollar store, craft store, or flea market, and then paint them the perfect shade to coordinate with your wool appliqué. If you don't want to frame your project, stitch the design to a premade pillow. Or add a hanging sleeve and make a wall hanging.

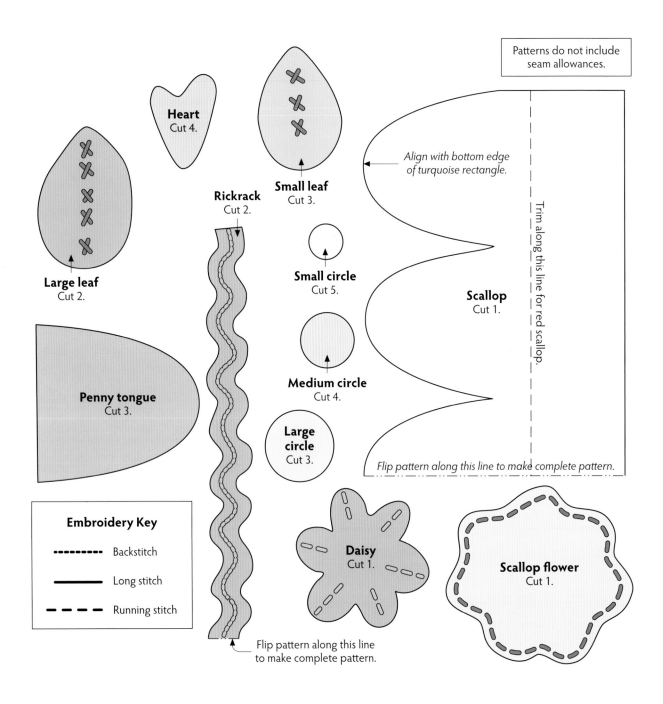

Heart
Cut 4.

Small leaf
Cut 3.

Large leaf
Cut 2.

Rickrack
Cut 2.

Small circle
Cut 5.

Medium circle
Cut 4.

Large circle
Cut 3.

Penny tongue
Cut 3.

Scallop
Cut 1.

Patterns do not include seam allowances.

Align with bottom edge of turquoise rectangle.

Trim along this line for red scallop.

Flip pattern along this line to make complete pattern.

Embroidery Key

- - - - - - - Backstitch

———— Long stitch

– – – – Running stitch

Flip pattern along this line to make complete pattern.

Daisy
Cut 1.

Scallop flower
Cut 1.

Letters
Cut 1 of each.

Wool-Appliqué Essentials

In this section you'll find all you need to know about making projects with wool appliqué—from the supplies you need to the stitches you'll use and more.

Wool-Appliqué Supplies

- Hand-dyed or felted 100% wool
- Small, sharp scissors
- Size #9 embroidery needles
- Embroidery floss
- Appliqué pins
- Fork pins
- Water-soluble basting glue, such as Roxanne's Glue-Baste-It
- Freezer paper
- Fusible web

Before You Begin

Here are some tips before you start.

- I use embroidery floss because it can be divided into strands. Use two strands of floss for blanket-stitching. Use one strand of floss for all other stitching, unless indicated otherwise. You can adjust the number of strands or use a thread you love to suit your look. See "Thread and Needles" (page 78).

- Freezer-paper templates are used for all of the designs except the letters. I use fusible web to stabilize letter shapes. The letter patterns in this book have been reversed for fusible appliqué.

- To keep the wool shapes from fraying, bring your floss up from the back to the front, in the background next to the appliqué shape, then stitch into the shape.

- Use a quilter's knot (or slipknot) to hide your knots inside the layers. When blanket-stitching two edges together, knot the floss and bring the needle up between the layers, catching the knot in the fibers. The needle will be at the edge of the shape. Make your first stitch, and then continue along the edge.

- Cut stems and vines freehand using scissors or a rotary cutter, whichever works best for you.

- For curved shapes, such as flowers, cut a circle around the shape close to the edges. Then snip down into the V and complete the curve.

- For stems and vines, draw a thin line using basting glue. Then lay the stem or vine on top of the glue.

Wool Basics

The beauty of wool work is that imperfections are expected and appreciated. Enjoy the fun and don't worry if your stitches are a little wonky. Most of these projects are made using scraps. Don't be afraid to use a wide variety of colors. A random color is often the perfect color! Hand-dyed wool is already felted and won't fray when cut. If the wool is off the bolt, you'll need to felt it before using it.

Felting Wool

To give 100% wool a thicker consistency, it needs to be felted before it can be used, especially for penny rugs and rug hooking. Felted wool doesn't fray and it has less stretch. Felted wool also gives a more uniform look to wool projects.

To felt wool, it needs to be submerged in hot water and agitated in order to allow the fibers to mesh together. To prevent the wool from rippling after felting, rip or cut off the selvage edges before washing.

1 Fill your washer with hot water and approximately one tablespoon of laundry detergent. Add your wool and optional fabric softener. Set the controls for a normal wash and rinse cycle.

2 Dry the wool in a medium to hot dryer for approximately 20 minutes. Do not overdry.

3 If the wool isn't thick enough to suit your needs, repeat steps 1 and 2 using hotter water. As a rule of thumb, if you're unsure about the weight of the wool, use a cooler temperature first.

Cutting Wool Shapes

When cutting out wool appliqués, you want to ensure that the cut pieces retain the shape of the design. Using freezer-paper templates helps keep the shapes consistent with the pattern. You can find freezer paper at your local quilt shop or grocery store. Freezer paper is two sided; one side is paper and the other side is waxy. Lay the freezer paper over your pattern and trace the designs onto the paper side, allowing about ½" between the pieces. Roughly cut all around each shape. With the wax side down and using a warm iron, press the pieces onto the appropriate wool colors. Cut out the pieces on the traced line. The templates can be reused several times.

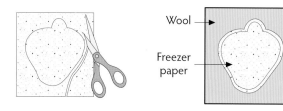

Wool

Freezer paper

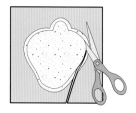

Basting Wool Appliqués

Position the wool appliqués on the background as described in the instructions for the project you are making. Then use one of the following methods to baste (or hold) the pieces in place.

- **Glass-head appliqué pins.** These pins are small and the thread won't catch on them as you stitch.

- **Staples.** Staples work especially well if the project will be transported, since they provide a secure hold.

- **Water-soluble adhesives, such as Roxanne's Glue-Baste-It.** Use small dots of glue to hold pieces firmly in place.

- **Fork pins.** Use these pins in the center of larger pieces to hold the back and front together. Then use appliqué pins along the edges.

Thread and Needles

You have a couple of thread choices for stitching wool projects.

- **Pearl cotton.** Pearl cotton is a twisted-ply thread that's available in several sizes. Often, the thicker sizes are used to finish the edges of penny rugs and circles.

- **Embroidery floss.** Floss comes in a variety of colors. It's easy to obtain, and you can easily separate it so that you can use as little as one strand or as many as six. Floss can be substituted for pearl cotton.

Use thin, sharp needles. I use a size #9 embroidery needle; it glides through the wool and makes stitching easy.

Wool-Appliqué Stitches

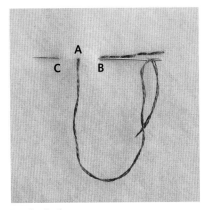

Backstitch

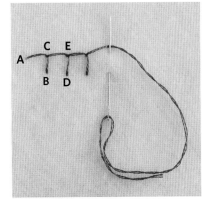

Blanket stitch

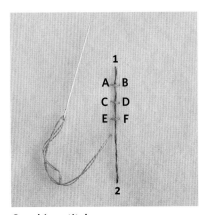

Couching stitch

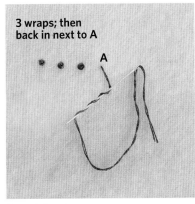

3 wraps; then back in next to A

French knot

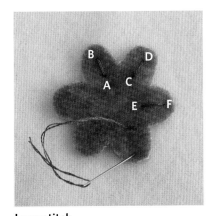

Long stitch

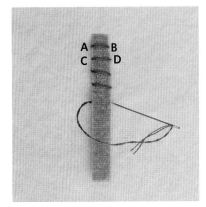

Overcast stitch

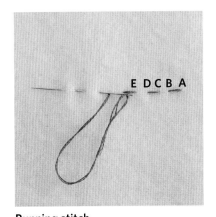

Running stitch

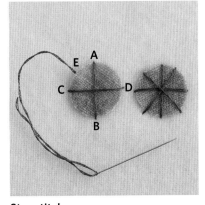

Star stitch

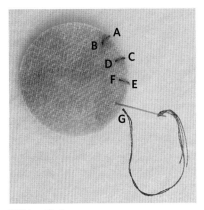

Whipstitch

Resources

I encourage you to support your local quilt shop. The following sites are resources for supplies if you can't find what you need locally.

Wool Vendors

Mary Flanagan Woolens
MFWoolens.com

Olympic Wool Works
OlympicWoolWorks.com

One Wing Wool
OneWingWool.com

Weeks Dye Works
WeeksDyeWorks.com

Wooly Lady
WoolyLady.com

Thread

Aurifil
Aurifil.com

DMC
dmc-usa.com

Valdani Inc.
Valdani.com

Other Supplies

Bohin France
Size #9 embroidery needles and size #22 tapestry needles
bohin.fr/en

Clover
Fork pins and glass-head appliqué pins
clover-usa.com

Colonial Needle
Roxanne's Glue-Baste-It
ColonialNeedle.com

Karen Kay Buckley
Curved scissors
KarenKayBuckley.com

Martingale
Kim Diehl's Best Appliqué Freezer Paper
ShopMartingale.com

OLFA
5" Precision scissors
Olfa.com

Redwork Plus
Embroidery needles and scissors
RedWorkPlus.com

Sizzix
Die-cutting machine and dies
Sizzix.com

Therm O Web
Feather lite fusible web
ThermOWeb.com

Thread Heaven
Thread conditioner
ThreadHeaven.com

Meet the Author

My mom was a 4-H leader for 38 years, and 4-H offered many learning opportunities. We could try a new subject each year, as long as we filled out the record books. In fact, 4-H is where my love affair with wool began. When I was nine years old, my first 4-H sewing project was a wool pincushion, stuffed with sawdust. I moved on to raising sheep at 13. At 17, I was a regional finalist in the Minnesota Make It Yourself with Wool competition, sporting a trendy wool cape. But it wasn't until I was a mom looking for a creative outlet that I fell in love with wool . . . again. I picked up a packet of small wool-appliqué designs, and from that moment on I was hooked.

As a history buff, I'm drawn to American folk art. And while I enjoy the coziness of the primitive look, I also love working with bright colors. It's amazing how they enhance each other. Add in thread and easy stitches, and appliqué shapes come to life.

Surrounding myself with a wool community has expanded my creativity. Whether it's wool meet-ups, a class, or my Muddy Sheep Wool Club meetings, there are talented wool workers who are always encouraging me to rise to a new level. Each time I see their work, my love affair with wool intensifies! To find out what's new, visit me at rosebuds-cottage.com.

~ Roseann Meehan Kermes